Other publications by Suzy Watson:

Norfolk Beaches Handbook

16 Coastal Dog Walks

If you want to find out more information on Norfolk, please visit the Explore Norfolk UK website at https://www.explorenorfolkuk.co.uk

NORFOLK
HERITAGE WALKS

18 Circular Walks With An Interest

By

Suzy Watson

Introduction

Norfolk is incredibly rich in history. It has a profusion of fascinating ruins, some very grand stately homes, and significant windmills, wind pumps and lighthouses; all are steeped in history and all have absorbing stories attached to them.

It made sense to try and bring this rich tapestry of life to you by putting together this Norfolk Heritage Walks book, and enabling you to follow the walks around or close to these wonderful sites and to discover something of historical interest for yourself. Many of these places are real Norfolk gems and often take the visitor by surprise, particularly some of the ruins.

There are 18 circular walks in this book and each one features a point of interest that played an important part in the lives of Norfolk dwellers many years ago. Each walk has a summary of the place of interest, with a little hint of its uniqueness, a postcode for the start of the walk, facilities available, whether there's an entry fee, whether the walk is dog friendly and most importantly, it includes detailed maps.

When I moved to Norfolk in 1992, I knew that there were many magnificent places to visit, so I set out to find circular walks that would include something with a little bit more of an interest other than just a path, road or track. I was keen to discover more about Norfolk (also known as Nelson's County) and its rich heritage.

With this book, you now have a perfect excuse to take a circular walk around the Norfolk countryside whilst learning something new about Norfolk's history; that's what I hope you gain from choosing some, or all of the many walks in this book.

A Potted History Of Norfolk

Norfolk dates back to the Ice Age which is verified by the discovery of tools and coins found near Snettisham, as well as the Pingo Ponds in and around Thompson in Mid Norfolk.

We then know that the Iceni tribe lived here before the Romans inhabited Norfolk; this is very apparent in the Peddars Way National Trail which used to be a Roman road running from Knettishall Heath right up to the coast, as well as Burgh Castle, details of which you will find in this book. After the Romans, Boudicca followed, after which the Anglo Saxons settled. Then came the Normans, and this is where Norfolk really came to the fore. Norwich grew into an important city and Norfolk gradually became the most densely populated region in England. I told you it was a potted history!

Churches were obviously central to medieval life, and the ruins of these monastic communities feature many times in this book; Walsingham Priory, Castle Acre Priory, Creake Abbey, Binham Priory and St Benet's Abbey.

During the 15th century a couple of large and stunning Tudor houses cropped up in Norfolk; Blickling Hall and Oxburgh Hall. Both of these houses feature in this book and are now managed by the National Trust.

In the 17th Century, the Jacobean era, Felbrigg Hall was built (now also managed by the National Trust). The church in the grounds has wonderful box pews and the largest collection of brasses in Norfolk.

The 18th Century produced some wonderful Georgian architecture, although the Palladian structure of Holkham Hall is often viewed as rather austere. From a distance though, it is staggering.

In the 19th Century Norfolk likes to boast about its links to Admiral Lord Nelson. He was born in Burnham Thorpe and learnt to sail on the creeks in North Norfolk. Unfortunately, he met his fate at the

Battle of Trafalgar.

History is always popping its head up in Norfolk, which is what makes it such an intriguing county.

A Few Discoveries

In 1998 "Seahenge"; a 4,000-year-old Bronze Age timber circle was discovered at Holme-next-the-Sea on the North Norfolk Coast.

In 1990 the remains of a Steppe Mammoth were discovered on West Runton Beach, again on the North Norfolk Coast.

In 2013, a team of scientists discovered a series of footprints in what would have been estuary mud dating back 800,000 years. They were discovered at low tide on Happisburgh beach, on the east coast of Norfolk.

The Artist

The artwork within the book is drawn by the talented artist, Will Assheton, (https://www.willasshetonartist.co.uk)

When I saw a drawing that he had created of St Paul's Cathedral, as well as one of Nelson's Column in London (Nelson being a Norfolk man), I was prompted to commission him to come to Norfolk and draw some of the historical buildings that feature in this book.

He has a real passion for structure and the aesthetics and this really shines through in his drawings.

He spent several days in Norfolk sketching the architecture and took them back to London to finalize. I really think they bring Norfolk history to life. He is also available for commissions, please visit his website.

The Maps

The maps have been superimposed from OS maps and are accurate in terms of scale but I have obviously had to reduce the size of the maps in order for them to fit on the pages.

This book, and the maps, are intended to provide information only. I cannot be held responsible for any alterations along the paths or any loss or damage arising from your reliance of this book. **An OS map is always advisable**, although most of these walks are very obvious.

Contents

Introduction 4

    A Potted History Of Norfolk 5

    A Few Discoveries.. 6

    The Artist.. 6

    The Maps 7

Map of the 18 Norfolk Heritage Walks 10

Walk 1. Burgh Castle (1.5 miles) 11

Walk 2. Happisburgh (3 miles)..................................... 15

Walk 3. Creake Abbey (3.5 miles) 20

Walk 4. Baconsthorpe Castle (3.5 miles) 24

Walk 5. West Raynham (4.2 miles)................................ 28

Walk 6. Walsingham (4.3 miles) 33

Walk 7. The Burnhams (4.5 miles)................................ 38

Walk 8. Binham Priory (4.5 miles)................................ 45

Walk 9. Blickling Hall (4.5 miles) 51

Walk 10. Felbrigg Hall (4.8 miles) 57

Walk 11. Oxburgh and Gooderstone walk (4.9 miles) ... 64

Walk 12. Bircham Windmill (5.1 miles) 69

Walk 13. Horsey Windpump (5 miles)........................... 74

Walk 14. Bawsey Ruin (5.6 miles)................................ 80

Walk 15. 3 possible walks to Ludham Bridge, St Benet's Abbey,
Toad Hole Museum and the How Hill Estate 85

    5.3 mile circular walk to St Benet's Abbey and Ludham Bridge 87

    6.3 mile walk to Ludham Bridge, Toad Hole and How Hill........ 91

    8.35 miles to St Benet's Abbey, Ludham Bridge, Toad Hole 96

Walk 16. Holkham Hall (6-7 miles) 101

Walk 17. Castle Acre Priory (6 miles) 106

Walk 18. Castle Rising (7 miles) 112

9

Map of the 18 Norfolk Heritage Walks

This map gives you a rough guide as to where the walks are located

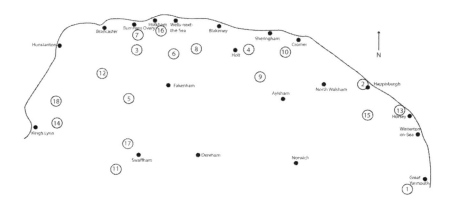

Walk 1. Burgh Castle (1.5 miles)

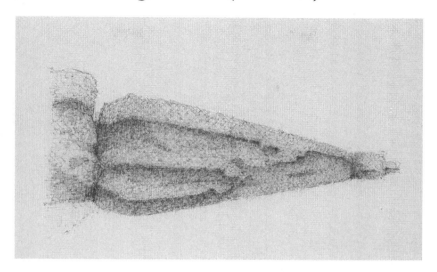

Burgh Castle is a very impressive thick-walled ruin of a Roman Fort just outside Great Yarmouth. It's a truly awe-inspiring moment the minute you see these huge walls of stone overlooking Breydon Water and the marshes. This particular fort is known as Gariannonum (a Saxon Shore fort) and was built to protect part of the Eastern coastline (also known as the Saxon Shore). Three imposing walls still remain standing and are really quite spectacular. The fourth wall fell into the marshes many years ago; something you'll understand when you visit and see how close these walls are to the reedbeds.

This is one of the best preserved forts in the UK and you can spend a long time just wandering around the grassy area of the interior walls and admiring the far-reaching views. This particular walk is a very simple walk with the paths clearly defined.

The surrounds of Burgh Castle are also rich in wildlife due to the marshland and the RSPB Breydon Water Nature Reserve which is the largest protected wetland in the UK.

ROUTE DIRECTIONS

Map Details: OS Explorer OL40

Postcode: NR31 9QB

Grading: Easy

What to expect: The impressive ruins of the Roman fort, far reaching views over the marshes and drainage mills, a board walk, the round tower church of St Peter and St Paul

Dog friendly: Yes

Length: 1.5 miles

Time: ½ - 1 ½ hours depending on how long you take to wander around the ruins

Start Location: Park in the free designated car par for Burgh Castle (in Butt Lane)

Facilities: None, but there is a pub in the village

Entry Cost: Free

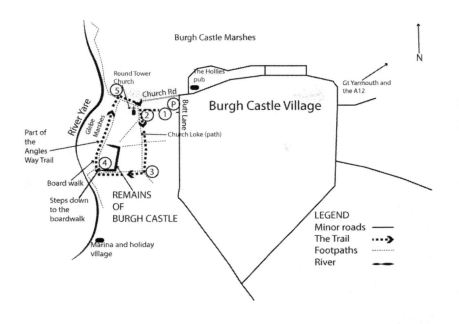

1. From the car park walk through the large metal kissing gate and turn right to follow the path which joins Church Loke path where you'll see the pretty round tower church in front of you. You may like to visit this before your walk.

2. Turn left to join the obvious path and continue straight ahead. As you walk along here, you'll see several entrances on your right which you can take to reach the ruins (if you wish), but with this walk you continue to follow the well-trodden path until you reach a sharp right hand corner.

3. Turn right here and walk towards the castle ruins and the marshes. Once at the ruins you can then take some time to wander around or just sit and admire the views.

4. Once you've reached the corner of the fort you will notice some steps going down towards the marshes and reed beds.

Take these steps down and turn immediately right to walk along the board walk. Don't deviate off the board walk unless you want a shorter walk, in which case you'll see a couple of steps off the board walk which take you back up the hill to the castle remains. This boardwalk is also a stretch of Angles Way. Walk all the way along the board walk until it ends at a junction.

5. Bear right, following the wooded path to a metal kissing gate. Once through here you'll see a grass triangle and the round tower church on your right. Walk through another gate on the other side of the grass triangle and re-trace your steps back to the car park.

Walk 2. Happisburgh (3 miles)

Happisburgh Lighthouse is one of the most iconic sights on the Norfolk landscape and is instantly recognizable by its red and white striped tower overlooking the eroding cliffs on the east coast of Norfolk. The reason it was painted red and white was to distinguish it in daylight from the lighthouse at Winterton-on-Sea (after the second Low Light lighthouse at Happisburgh was demolished in 1883 due to coastal erosion).

This lighthouse was built in 1790 after a severe winter storm which caused the loss of 70 ships and 600 men. An inquiry was held which drew attention to the fact that there were no warning lights between a fire beacon at Cromer and a candle powered light at Winterton. It is

15

one of the oldest working lighthouses and the only independently run lighthouse in the UK.

If you take this walk on the same day as an open day, you will be able to walk right up to the top of the lighthouse, as well as walking up to the top of St Mary's church tower (which is in the middle of Happisburgh and en route.

There are two other reason I have included this heritage walk in the book.

First, in 2010, a discovery of over 70 flint axes were discovered on Happisburgh beach which pre-dated the first known occupation of humans in the UK by 250,000 years.

The second is that in 2013, approximately 50 footprints were exposed on the beach at low tide dating back 800,000 years. They are the oldest known human footprints to be discovered outside Africa. Luckily, they were photographed in 3D before they were washed away by the tide.

ROUTE DIRECTIONS

Map Details: OS Explorer 252

Postcode: The nearest postcode is NR12 0PR but it is also fairly well signposted

Grading: Easy

What to expect: The iconic red and white striped lighthouse, St Mary's Church, a stretch of the Norfolk Coast Path, coastal erosion

Dog friendly: Yes

Length: 3 miles

Time: 1¼ hours

Start Location: Happisburgh Lighthouse car park at the end of Beach Road – this is a pay and display machine operated car park

Facilities: WC, playground. There is a pub in the village

Entry Cost: You can only go into the Lighthouse on open days for a charge, but you can walk right around the bottom of it at any time of year

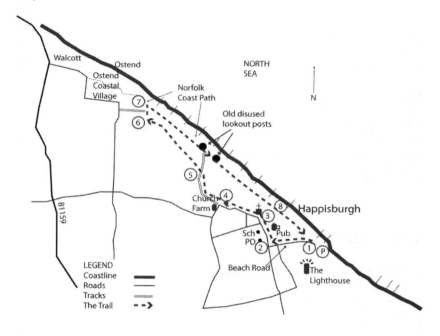

1. Park at the Happisburgh Lighthouse car park on Beach Road. Walk out of the car park and down Beach Road towards the village.

2. At the T Junction, cross over the road and turn right, heading towards the church, passing the local school on your left. At the sharp corner, walk straight over the main road and join a

little lane heading up towards the church.

3. Just before you reach the church, follow the road round to the left, walking down the slight incline. Continue along this road, passing the graveyard on your right and a recreation ground on your left.

4. Eventually the road turns sharply left. At this corner, continue straight ahead along a gravel track with Church Farm on your left. Continue along this track with views over the open countryside, passing another house and farm buildings until you reach a metal gate.

5. Just after the metal gate you'll see a wide track on the left through the field, running parallel with the coast. At this stage you could take a shorter walk by walking on through the gate and reaching the lookout posts. It cuts the walk short by one mile, but it's much nicer to continue for a longer stretch on the cliffs of the Norfolk Coast Path. To continue the original walk, follow the footpath through the field, joining another path which takes you along the edge of a field heading towards Walcott.

6. Just before a corner in the field (which is obvious), look out for a little sign and footpath to the right which cuts diagonally through another field heading towards the coast. You don't want to carry on to the houses. The path you take is a well-trodden narrow path which eventually takes you onto the Norfolk Coast Path. A little bit of common sense is required here (i.e. follow the footpath to the coastal cliffs!)

7. Once at the cliffs, you have now joined the Norfolk Coast Path. Turn right and walk all the way along here where you'll see the church in the distance and the wooden coastal defenses on the beach below. You'll also pass two derelict

lookout posts.

8. Continue along here, following the Norfolk Coast Path signs, through an old caravan park and continue in the same direction, joining a grassy field with another well-trodden path. You will come out onto the road you started on. Turn left and you'll see the car park on your right.

Walk 3. Creake Abbey (3.5 miles)

Creake Abbey is a small but very pretty priory ruin dedicated to St Mary of the Meadows in the heart of Norfolk. It originally belonged to the Augustinian Canons who were the most popular of all the religious orders in Norfolk.

It was founded in 1206, and in 1217 it was transformed into a hospital with 13 beds for "Christian paupers". 10 years later it became a Priory to which King Henry III became Patron. Due to the royal connections, it was then granted Abbey status (a church that's part of a monastery) and thrived for 250 years.

In 1484 a fire took hold, and further sorrow befell the Abbey. It was reduced in size to a small church, the Canons succumbed to the Plague and the Abbot finally died in 1506. At this point the property passed to the Crown and was eventually used for farming purposes. Creake Abbey ruins are managed by English Heritage and the monastic buildings and cloister are now private property, but you can however, freely wander around the ruins.

Today it sits adjacent to a small enterprise including a few independent shops, a gallery and a wonderful food hall and café.

ROUTE DIRECTIONS

Map Details: OS Explorer 251

Postcode: NR21 9LF

Grading: Easy

What to expect: The 11th century ruins of St Mary of The Meadow (also known as Creake Abbey ruins), peaceful farm tracks and typical Norfolk countryside with far reaching views, the flintstone village of North Creake

Dog friendly: Yes, if you don't mind a little bit of road walking between points 5 and 8 on the map

Length: 3.5 miles

Time: 1 ½ hours

Start Location: Park just outside Creake Abbey ruins (free). Access to the ruins is along the left-hand fork of the drive for Creake Abbey Food Hall and Café

Facilities: Creake Abbey Café and Food Hall. Car parking also available here

Entry Cost: Free

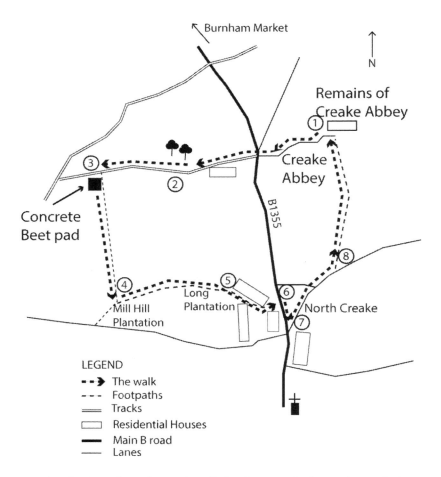

1. Park at the ruins and walk back towards the main road, the same way you came in. Cross straight over the main B1355 and walk along the farm track (Crossways Farm), passing the farmhouse set back on your left and continue along this undulating quiet track with hedges on either side.

2. Pass a small woodland on your right and continue up the slight incline until you see a large gap in the hedges on the left with a concrete beet pad and beyond that, a grassy track. The track has a hedgerow on the left.

22

3. Turn left and walk all the way along this grassy undulating track with far reaching views over the rolling countryside. At the far end of this field you will reach a farm track "T junction".

4. Turn left here to continue along more track with a tiny plantation on your right and a hedge on your left. Follow this all the way until you meet the tarmac road in the village with a playground straight in front of you.

5. Continuing in the same direction, join the tarmac road heading slightly down the hill (Duns Lane) until you reach a T junction.

6. Turn right here, walking along the pavement and admiring the flint stone cottages.

7. Once you reach the pub (The Jolly Farmer) on your right, take the sharp left-hand road (towards Wells) almost coming back on yourself, crossing the little stream with white railings. Walk along this road, rising gently, passing a grass triangle with a lone tree and a circular seat around it.

8. When you're almost at the brow of the hill, look out for a wide grass public bridleway track to your left. Turn left along this peaceful track until you arrive back at the Creake Abbey Farm and the Priory ruins.

Walk 4. Baconsthorpe Castle (3.5 miles)

Baconsthorpe Castle is a little gem hidden away in North Norfolk. The peace and tranquility that surrounds this area is second to none.

These ruins comprise a moated and fortified 15th century gatehouse which, at the time, was an indication of great extravagance and wealth in a family.

Work started on the site of a former manor in 1450 by the Heydon family. In later years, in order to protect their manor, a castle was then built around the manor and an outer gatehouse was also added.

However, 200 years later, financial difficulties meant that they had to demolish parts of the castle and gatehouse, selling many of the building materials for money.

It sits in a beautiful setting, partly surrounded by a lake and is managed by English Heritage. There are also various information boards dotted around the ruins which provide interesting reading.

ROUTE DIRECTIONS

Map Details: OS Explorer 252

Postcode: NR25 9LN

Grading: Easy but with stiles

What to expect: The ruins of the 15th century Baconsthorpe Castle, peaceful countryside tracks, fields and quiet lanes

Dog friendly: Yes, if you don't mind a little bit of road walking between points 6 and 7 on the map. *There is also quite a large stile to negotiate with a big dog* (see photo at the end of this walk)

Length: 3.5 miles

Time: 1 ½ hours

Start Location: Park just outside the Baconsthorpe Castle Ruins (free)

Entry Cost: Free

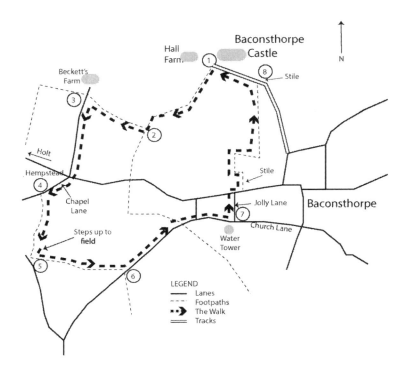

1. Start the walk with your back to the Castle. Walk over the cattle grid and bear right and then turn left to follow the track away from the castle, keeping the hedge on your right.

2. At a junction in the path, take the right-hand track (don't carry straight on) and head along this lovely quiet path until you reach the tarmac lane and a house in front of you.

3. Turn left here and walk along this lane until you reach a crossroads with the main road. Walk straight over the road along Chapel Lane and up the slight incline.

26

4.   Just before you reach the sign for Hempstead, take a grassy track on your left, keeping the row of trees and hedge on your right. Walk down this track until you reach another tarmac road.

5.   Just before this road, you'll see some steps up into the field on your left. Take these steps and follow the path cutting through the large field to reach another tarmac lane.

6.   Once here, turn left and walk along the quiet lane, heading towards the water tower, until you reach Baconsthorpe.

7.   Take the 2nd left hand turn down Jolly Lane (opposite the water tower). Turn right at the T junction along the main road (The Street) and then about 30 yards on your left you'll see a small track. Take this track and cross over the stile and follow the path all the way around the fields (the track is obvious). At the corner of one of the fields is a wooden footbridge on your left (which you'll see and is also signposted). Walk over this bridge and continue along the path (which can have quite long grass in the summer months) until you reach another stile which brings you out onto the tarmac track back to the Castle.

8.   Turn left here and head back to the Castle.

Walk 5.   West Raynham (4.2 miles)

R aynham Hall is a magnificent 17th Century country house and has been home to the Townshend family for about 400 years. It is set back from the road with a beautiful tree lined drive which you will walk past. The house is reported to be haunted and is the location of one of the most famous ghost photographs "The Brown Lady of Raynham Hall".

The ruins of St Margaret's Church, also known as Little Raynham Church, are three quarters of the way around the walk. It's a fascinating ruin in that it still has a font in amongst the ruins, as well as a brick-built altar, and the church is still occasionally used today. It fell to ruins and was abandoned in the 18th century when the lead was used to pay for the restoration of St Mary's Church in East Raynham, which you will also walk past.

ROUTE DIRECTIONS

Map Details: OS Explorer 238

Postcode: NR21 7AH

Grading: Easy

What to expect: This walk takes in part of the pretty Raynham Estate, the ruins of St Mary's Church, as well as walking along the chalk stream river of the Wensum. *COWS are in one of the fields so best without dogs*

Dog friendly: No

Length: 4.2 miles

Time: 1½ - 2 hours

Start Location: In the village of Helhoughton, opposite the church

Facilities: None

Entry Cost: Not applicable

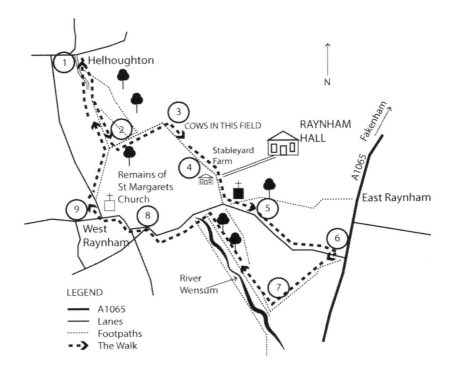

1. Park by the church. Keeping the church on your left, walk in an easterly direction to the end of the houses which are on your right. Turn right here and walk down the field keeping the post and wire fence on your left (and a few houses and their driveway on your right).

2. Hug the fence and bear left at the end of this field along a wide farm track. Take this path into the wooded area with a thin reed bed on your right until you reach a metal fence with a kissing gate into a field of cows.

3. **If you don't like cows, this probably isn't a good walk for you. I've been once in the summer when the cows took no notice of you, and once at calving time which was very interesting and a little frightening. So, choose your time**

carefully. It is a footpath though so there shouldn't really be any problems.

4. Turn immediately right in the field and walk along the side of the fence to the metal gate in the far diagonal corner. Walk through the working farmyard and follow the drive all the way to the church. You'll notice the pretty gables on the houses and the impressive long barn as you pass through here. You'll also walk past the tree-lined drive to the beautiful Raynham Hall.

5. Walk past the church and out of the gates, turning left along the road, walking up the tree-lined incline to the top of the hill. Continue along this road.

6. Just before you meet the main A1065 and a house in front of you, turn right, taking the footpath in front of the house and walk diagonally back down through the field (a well-trodden path is marked here). Follow this path all the way to the river and a wooden bridge.

7. Get to the bridge, don't go over it, but turn right along this pretty path into the wooded area and follow it all the way to the road (keeping the river on your left). Once at the road, turn left walking into West Raynham village along the peaceful Estate road.

8. At the village sign, take the right-hand fork and turn right at the T junction. A little way along here, you'll see the ruins of St Mary's Church on the right, located through a wooden gate with a cross above it. Returning to the walk, once out of the gates turn right and continue along the main road passing a playground on your right and bear sharp right following the road.

9. Walk down the slight incline to the first large gap in the hedge (on the right) and walk diagonally across the open field (well-trodden path) until you reach the post and wire fence which you walked along at the beginning of the walk. Retrace your steps here and walk back towards Helhoughton.

Walk 6.   Walsingham (4.3 miles)

Walsingham Priory and the village of Little and Great Walsingham are world renowned for the great pilgrimage that is walked every year by around 250,000 pilgrims. This particular walk is a perfect excuse to visit the historic remains of Walsingham Priory, as well as the village of Lt Walsingham which has been recognized as one of the holiest places in England.

The magnificent and impressive East window is pretty much all that is left of this Augustinian Priory, but there are also a few other remaining relics such as the refectory and the west tower, two wells and a bath as well as the crypt which has a wonderful vaulted ceiling.

One of the very best times to visit here is in February when the grounds are covered in a beautiful carpet of snowdrops.

Walsingham village is a wonderful historic village with many timbered buildings as well as the Norman arch of the Priory which you'll walk right past on this walk.

ROUTE DIRECTIONS

Map Details: OS Explorer 251

Postcode: Nearest postcode NR22 6DH

Grading: Easy

What to expect: Walsingham Priory, countryside, flint stone villages, The Slipper Chapel where the Roman Catholic shrine of Our Lady Of Walsingham sits, part of the Pilgrims Way route, crossing a ford, a stretch of a busy lane without pavement

Dog friendly: Unadvisable, as there are sheep in one field and there is quite a busy lane to walk along without any pavement

Length: 4.3 miles

Time: 1½ hours

Start Location: The Old Mill car park in the centre of Gt Walsingham village, easily distinguished by the chimney of an old mill

Facilities: Two pubs in the village, farm shop and stores. W.C. in the middle of the village adjacent to the medieval Abbey Gatehouse

Entry Cost: Charge to enter the Priory grounds if you wish to visit here and car parking charges with a pay and display machine

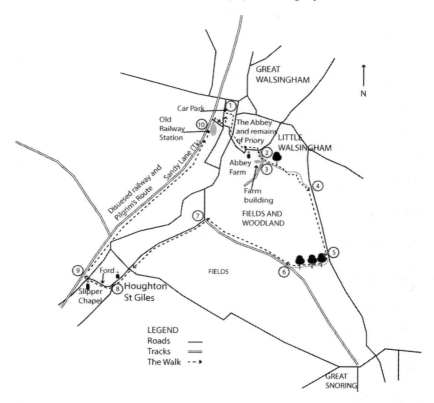

1. Walk out of the bottom of the car park, down the hill towards the middle of the village. Turn right to amble through the middle of the High Street. Walk to the bottom of this road passing various shrine shops along the way, and take the first left, Church Street. Follow this road until you come face to face with village church and its splendid flint stone wall. Continue to follow the road which wiggles to the left and then right until you arrive at a wrought iron gate on

your left with the Priory in view.

2. Opposite this gate is a farm track on your right. Take the track for a short distance following the wrought iron fence until you reach farm buildings on you right. Opposite these buildings is a gate and footpath sign taking you left into the field.

3. Go through the gate and head up the middle of the field to the top of the hill. **This field may well have sheep in it.** Pass one large oak tree on your left and continue until you reach a smaller tree and you find yourself in a dip. Walk up from the dip at the top of the field and bear diagonally right. Walk towards a lone telegraph pole and head down to the far right hand corner of the field where there is a gate and a stile.

4. Walk out of the field on to the road and turn right, walking for a while up the hill and beyond. Eventually you'll come across a large grassy/muddy farm track on your right with a row of trees on the left of this track. This is a short cut to get you across to the next path. (At this point, you'll see that the lane that you've been walking along starts to go gently downhill. If you start going downhill you've gone too far and you'll reach Great Snoring).

5. Turn right along this muddy farm track (keeping the trees on your left) and walk to the end of this field where you join another track (very obvious).

6. Turn right along this new track heading down the hill which is lined with trees and hedges on either side. It's very peaceful and tranquil.

7. Once at the bottom of this track you arrive at a lane. Turn left here and continue to walk all the way into Houghton St Giles. It can get a little busy and is quite narrow so beware of cars. However, the view to the right is lovely with the River Stiffkey winding its way towards Walsingham. Walk through the village, passing the first crossroads, and continue ahead in the direction of Fakenham.

8. Pass a small church on your right and take the next right which is a small lane heading down towards a ford. Continue over the ford and your reach a T junction. (The Slipper Chapel is a short distance down this road on the left).

9. Cross straight over the road for a very short distance and you will then reach the old railway line. This forms part of the Rosary Way and the Pilgrim Way. This stretch of the Pilgrim Way is supposed to have been done barefoot! Continue all the way along this track until it reaches a tarmac lane. The track also has a post in the middle of it to stop cars driving down.

10. Continue straight along the tarmac lane until you reach the old station platform and a house on the right which would have been the station building. Immediately after the end of the platform (which is obvious) and the metal fence, turn right and head down the hill towards the village. Take the first left and continue to walk along there until you arrive back at the car park.

Walk 7.   The Burnhams (4.5 miles)

The Burnham's circular walk is an important heritage walk to include in this book for the simple reason that Admiral Horatio Nelson was born in Norfolk in 1758 in the rectory at Burnham Thorpe, a village just south of where this walk takes you.

Norfolk is known as Nelson's County. He was Britain's greatest Naval Commander of all time and learnt to sail on the creeks and sea around North Norfolk. At aged 12 he joined his first ship, HMS Raisonnable and apparently suffered awful sea sickness! He was hit above his right eye in the Battle of the Nile and although he didn't lose his eye, he did lose his sight. And the loss of his right arm occurred during a fight at Santa Cruz in Tenerife in 1797 when he was shot with a musket ball around his right elbow and the surgeon had no option but to amputate his arm. Finally, during the Battle of Trafalgar he was shot through the shoulder and spine and later died.

This walk includes one of the 124 beautiful round tower churches as well as the ruins of St Mary's Friary in Burnham Norton. You can still see the 14th century gatehouse which was the main entrance to the Friary, and the room above was used as the chapel. It was more than likely used for a resting place for the Friars on their way to the shrine at Walsingham.

There used to be seven Burnham villages in North Norfolk, but over time three of the small villages merged into one to make Burnham Market, leaving six Burnham's in all. You will walk through four of them on this trail.

ROUTE DIRECTIONS

Map Details: OS Explorer 251

Postcode: PE31 8JF.

Grading: Easy

What to expect: St Mary's Friary, a round tower church and a church with an unusual bell tower, Commonwealth War Graves, farm tracks, Burnham Overy Windmill, a small stretch of the Norfolk Coast Path and amazing views towards the coast

Dog friendly: Yes, *if you don't mind some road walking* - (there is a small stretch of road walking along the B1155 heading towards Burnham Market and in Burnham Norton as well as at the end of the walk along the A149, but there is a pavement on all of these roads)

Length: 4.5 miles

Time: 1½ - 2 hours

Start Location: You can park at Burnham Overy Staithe harbour car park or along the roadside by the harbour, but beware of the tide times. If it's a high Spring tide you would be best to park away from the harbour car park

Facilities: The Hero pub in Burnham Overy Staithe

Entry Cost: Not applicable

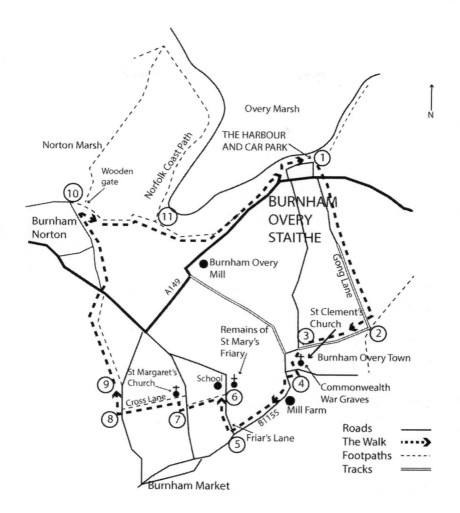

1. Park in Burnham Overy Staithe and walk away from the harbour heading inland along East Harbour Way. Walk straight over the main A149 (the Hero pub is on the corner of this road) and up along Gong Lane. Eventually the houses stop and you continue along a track with hedges on either side. This wiggles down a gentle slope.

2. Just before Burnham Overy Town (ahead), the track continues but there is also a grassy track to your right with

high hedges either side (this is obvious). Take this grassy track to the right, rather than continuing onto the village.

3. Walk to the end of the track and you'll see St Clement's Church with an unusual bell tower to the left. The graveyard is part of the Commonwealth War Graves. Turn left before the houses to walk along the grassy track towards the church, keeping the houses on your right. Walk around the church and out of the churchyard onto the lane.

4. Turn right here and walk down to the triangle. Follow the road round to the left heading towards Burnham Market. This is a very small stretch without pavement, but once around the corner you'll be able to walk along the pavement. Continue along the busy main A149, passing Mill Farm on your left.

5. Continue along here until you reach Friars Lane on your right. Cross over the road and walk along Friars Lane, up the slight incline, all the way to the remains of the Friary which you can visit. It's opposite the local school, and you'll also see Burnham Overy Staithe windmill in the distance.

6. Having visited the Friary, continue with your walk by turning left out of the Friary gates, cross the road and turn right along a narrow path with hedges on either side and with the school playing field on your right. Follow this path all the way until you reach a small lane. Turn right along the lane until you reach the pretty round tower church of St Margaret's, Burnham Market.

7. Take the left-hand track just before the church and continue along here until you reach another lane.

8. Turn right onto this lane and walk down the hill passing a gravel car park for St Margaret's Church on the right-hand side.

9. A little bit further past this you will see a gap in the hedge on the left-hand side where there is a footpath which takes you all the way down the side of the field to a tarmac road. There are fantastic views here towards the coast. Take this footpath to the bottom of the hill. Cross straight over the road and head at an angle along Norton Street into Burnham Norton. Continue to walk into the pretty flint stone village, passing an old red telephone box which is now used as a library.

10. The road eventually forks. Take the right-hand fork along a track leading to the marshes and reedbeds, with a house on your right. Walk through the wooden gate and follow the

path all the way until you join the Norfolk Coast Path. You'll be able to see Burnham Overy windmill in the distance.

11. Once on the Norfolk Coast Path follow the signs heading diagonally through the field, the windmill just above you. Continue along the side of the hedge until you come out onto the pavement. Follow the road and take the first left heading down towards the harbour to arrive back at where you started.

The ceiling in The Friary

Walk 8. Binham Priory (4.5 miles)

B inham Priory is one of the most spectacular priory ruins that you'll see in Norfolk (apart from Castle Acre Priory!). Building started in 1091 and took approximately 150 years to build. It housed just 14 Benedictine Monks for around 400 years. As with many priories, it was dissolved by Henry VIII in 1539. Much of the Priory was dismantled after the dissolution and the timbers and lead were sold. However, the church was left alone, and this is still in use today. You can feel free to wander inside and have a look. It has three wonderful tiered arched windows and beautiful carved pews. The church also displays many fascinating archaeological finds that were discovered on the site which are contained in purpose-built cabinets.

The ruins are managed by English Heritage and there are information boards dotted around the grounds which give you an understanding of how the Priory would have been when it was intact.

The village of Binham is a very traditional flint stone Norfolk village with a pub, a butcher and a local shop.

ROUTE DIRECTIONS

Map Details: OS Explorer 251

Postcode: NR21 0DQ

Grading: Easy with one slight incline

What to expect: The impressive ruins of the monastic Benedictine Priory and the Priory Church, peaceful Norfolk countryside with far reaching views along quiet lanes and farm tracks, 2 stiles, a pretty stream

Dog friendly: No, as there are stiles and meadowland with horses

Length: 4.5 miles

Time: 1 ½ - 2hrs

Start Location: Binham Priory car park (free)

Facilities: The ruins are open all day during reasonable daylight hours but the church has restricted opening times – in the summer 9am-6pm and winter is 9am-4pm. Dogs on leads are allowed in the ruins. WC is available in the church when open

Entry Cost: Free

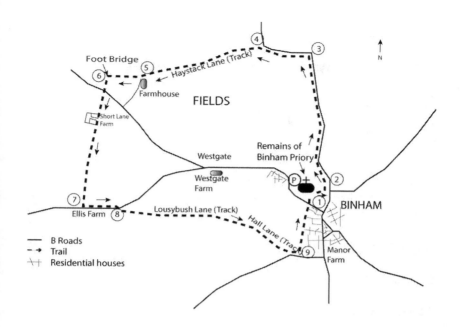

1. Park at the English Heritage Binham Priory car park. Walk
    through either gate to reach the impressive ruins. Keeping
    the church building and the priory column ruins on your left,
    you'll see a gate straight ahead. Walk through the metal gate
    into the field and head straight across towards the houses on
    the far side and you'll come out to a quiet lane. Turn left
    onto this lane.

    (WARNING: sometimes there are cattle in this field so if
    you don't like the idea of walking in a field of cows the
    alternative is to walk out of the fenced area of ruins, turn left
    and head towards the flint wall where you'll see a gate.
    Walk through the gate, turn left onto the main road and head
    down the hill into the village. At the road junction at the
    bottom of the hill, turn left signed to Langham and walk
    along the main road for a short distance. As the road bears
    round to the right, you continue straight ahead along a quiet
    lane signposted to Stiffkey).

2. Continue along this road, heading up the hill and away from the village.

3. At the top of the hill, follow the road round to the left.

4. When the road bears round to the right, you continue straight ahead along the farm track with low hedges on either side. There are lovely far reaching views across the open countryside from here. This track continues for a while, eventually passing a farm house set back from the track.

5. Carry on walking straight ahead to a gate and a grassy meadow. Walk through this meadow, alongside the hedge on your right, until you reach a wooden bridge crossing a pretty stream.

6. Cross over the bridge and walk directly ahead through the meadow, crossing over a little stone bridge half way across the field and head towards another quiet lane. Once at the lane, cross straight ahead and continue along the tarmac road, passing Short Lane Farm on your right. The tarmac becomes a grassy track alongside a large open field.

Continue along here until you reach another lane.

7. Turn left here, passing Ellis Farm on your right and walk until you reach a slight left-hand bend in the road.

8. At this point, look out for the signpost and track on the right which heads into a field between a hedge and trees. Walk along the short line of trees (keeping them on your left) until you get to the end of them, and then head directly across the field where there is a cleared cross-track path towards a hedge at the top of the field. This meandering track takes you all the way to a lane in Binham village. You get quite a good view of the Binham church bell tower and window from here.

9. Walk out on to the lane and a little way along here on the left (approx. 50 yds), just after the Binham sign, is a grassy track. Turn left down here, walking past houses on your right, until you reach a gap in the flintstone wall which opens up to an obvious residential car park belonging to converted barn residences. Walk straight through this and you'll arrive at the main road. Cross the road, through the gate and you are back at Binham Priory.

Walk 9. Blickling Hall (4.5 miles)

Blickling Hall is a stunning and fascinating 15th century National Trust property with magnificent grounds to wander around, a stunning lake that looks onto the house and an beautiful formal garden.

It was originally owned by Sir John Falstaf of Caister from 1380-1459 (he also built Caister Castle). It then changed hands to the Boleyn family, their most famous daughter being Anne Boleyn, one of the wives of Henry VIII. It's believed she was born at Blickling Hall, but there are no official documents to back this up. Legend also has it that there are three ghosts who patrol the house and gardens here! The present house was designed in 1616 and was actually built on the ruins of the original site.

During WWII it was used as an Officers Mess from nearby RAF Oulton and eventually passed into the hands of the National Trust where it remains today.

ROUTE DIRECTIONS

Map Details: OS Explorer 252

Postcode: NR11 6NF

Grading: Easy

What to expect: Beautiful countryside and ancient woodland, estate church, ice house, The Tower, a lake, extraordinary 1794 pyramid mausoleum, carpets of bluebells (in April/May). Stunning house and formal gardens

Dog friendly: No, if you want to visit the house and gardens. Yes, if you're just walking in the grounds

Length: 4.5 miles

Time: 2 hours

Start Location: National Trust Blickling Hall Car park (National Trust fees, members free)

Facilities: Café, WC

Entry Cost: National Trust fee for car park and house

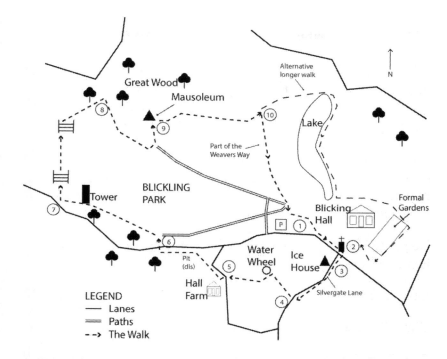

1. From the main car park, face the visitor centre and take the path on the left-hand side of the centre to walk down to the lane. Notice the top of Blickling Hall from here. Follow the signs to the house, pass the pub and admire the view of the house from the front gates!

2. Continue ahead to the church. Walk through the church yard, pop in and see the wonderful marble tomb and then walk to the far right hand corner of the church yard. Cross the road and head along the quiet lane (Silvergate Lane and also signposted Weavers Way).

3. Just along here, on the right and at the end of the post and rail fence, you can nip into the wood and see the 18th Century Ice House (a small mound and under quite a bit of ivy). Used until the 1930's, it's a Grade II listed building.

4. Continue along the lane for about a third of a mile until you see a way marker with an orange arrow and a stile in the hedge on the right-hand side. Climb over this stile and the next stile (dogs can get under these), and walk straight ahead to the small brick building. This is an old pump house which used to pump water to the house. Climb over that stile too and follow the path through the woodland, out onto the edge of the field until you come to an opening in the hedge on the left and you reach a tarmac lane, opposite Hall Farm. The tracks are obvious.

5. Turn right onto this lane for 100 meters or so and look for the way marker and a track on your left. Take this left track, passing a cottage and follow the path. Just before you reach the main road, turn left along the path that runs parallel to the road, and continue to walk through the wood.

6. The path takes you across the main road. Cross this road and walk around the first gate in front of you. Just **before** the 2nd gate, there is a wide path on your left. Take this path and follow it all the way until you reach The Tower, which is obvious to see when you reach it. The Tower is now a holiday cottage, but it was built in the 18th century as a grandstand for the steeple chase racecourse which ran across the area now known as Tower Park.

Continue to follow the path, keeping The Tower and the fields on your right. When you almost reach the main road, **ignore the path going straight on** (Buck's Common).

7. Turn sharp right alongside the post and wire fence, with the

meadow on your right and the woods on your left. Go through the gate at the end, walk straight over the meadow, cross another small section of wood and head towards another gate. Go through the gate and follow the sign which takes you right and down alongside Bunker's Hill Plantation towards Great Wood. (Great Wood is little changed since the 18th Century with a mix of Oak, Beech and Sweet Chestnuts as well as some fabulous bluebells in Spring.

8. Follow the path to the right, following the way markers. Walk up the hill until the path forks and you reach the 2nd seat on the left (also pass one on the right). From here you could carry on straight ahead and end up back at the car park. However, for a longer walk, turn left at the fork and follow the path until you reach an opening where you'll see the Mausoleum on the left. This was built in 1794 in the shape of a large pyramid to house the remains of the 2nd Earl of Buckinghamshire and his two wives

9. With the Mausoleum behind you, walk straight ahead, over the 1st path and take the 2nd path veering to the left (by a huge oak tree and seat). Follow this path, which bears right and comes into open countryside. Lovely views over the Norfolk countryside.

10. Once in the woods, turn right towards a gate (and this path is also part of the Weaver's Way). Head downhill through the parkland, with the lake on your left, until you reach the white gates. Walk through these, bear left and the car park is on the right. If you wanted an even longer walk, you could carry on when you reach the woods, and walk all the way around the lake and the back of Blickling Hall.

Walk 10. Felbrigg Hall (4.8 miles)

Felbrigg Hall is a 17th century Jacobean stately home owned by the National Trust. Felbrigg Hall is architecturally interesting due to the increased wealth of the four Norfolk families who lived there, generation after generation.

There are some fascinating rooms to visit in the Hall such as the gothic style library where all of the 5,000 original books still sit, a kitchen with all the shiny brass pots and pans hanging from the dresser, and an extraordinary slipper bath.

Outside there is a beautiful walled garden, vast parkland and woodlands and this walk has the bonus of two unusual church interiors. One is on the estate grounds which has box pews, the other is at Sustead, one of Norfolk's 124 round tower churches, with a most unusual interior ceiling.

ROUTE DIRECTIONS

Map Details: OS Explorer 252

Postcode: NR11 8PP

Grading: Easy

What to expect: Jacobean Felbrigg Hall, the Estate church with box pews, Sustead round tower church with an unusual ceiling, wide open countryside and mature woodland, Felbrigg Hall lake, peace and tranquility during the walk

Dog friendly: Yes, if you are prepared to have your dogs on leads for some of the walk due to livestock in field; they must be under control

Length: 4.8 miles

Time: 1 ¾ hours

Start Location: The National Trust Felbrigg Hall car park where there is a pay and display machine. National Trust members are free.

Facilities: W.C and a café in the courtyard at Felbrigg Hall (free entry apart from the car park charge)

Entry Cost: There is a price for a whole site admission. However, the parkland is free and open from dawn till dusk so you can walk this at any time. There is a charge for the car park of approx. £3 for the day. National Trust Members are free. The Hall, walled garden shop and Squires pantry have limited opening hours. Please refer to the Felbrigg Hall website for this if you want to visit the property

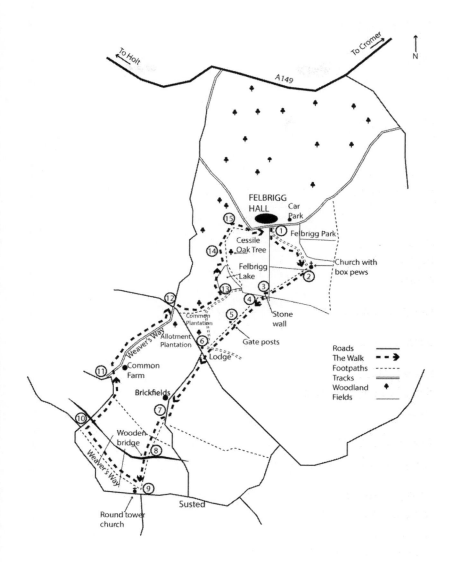

1. Start in the National Trust car park. As you look towards the
    house you will see park land and the church to your left. You
    will also see a small wooden gate with a path that takes you
    towards this church. Head towards the church and you

might like to pop inside as there are some very unusual box pews.

2. Walk out of the church gates and turn left, heading towards another wooden gate. Walk through this gate and turn right to walk diagonally up and across the field to the far end where you will see another gate.

3. Once through the gate at the top of the hill (admire the view of the Hall to your right in the distance), turn left and walk through the stone wall turning immediately right down the hill for a short distance.

4. Where the stone wall ends, bear left crossing the field diagonally down the hill to walk between 2 gate posts. (Don't walk to the lake at the bottom of the hill, you will come back to this later).

5. Once through the gate posts bear left diagonally up the hill towards the woods where you will see another gate.

6. Walk through this gate and follow the short path bearing left towards a house and from here you will see a tarmac lane. Cross straight over the road and continue along the lane heading up the hill. Pass Brickfield House on your right and continue along the road.

7. Just before the lane bears round to the left you will see a large gap in the hedge on the right which opens up to a field. Go through this gap and bear left walking diagonally through the field. You will see the obvious footpath. Cross this field which heads slightly downhill and go through the gate at the end of the field.

8. Bear slightly right and head towards a wooden bridge on your left. Cross over this bridge and head up the hill towards the church. This is the round tower church of St Peter and St Paul, Sustead, and worth visiting as it has a very unusual ceiling above the altar.

9. To continue the walk, retrace your steps back into the field walking down one side of the flintstone wall surrounding the church. At the corner of the church wall, bear left diagonally across the field. This is now following the Weavers Way trail and is well signposted. Walk across three fields until you reach a lane.

10. At the lane turn right and continue along this road.

11. The road bends sharply to the left, continue to follow this road until you reach Common Farm on the right-hand side which is well signposted. There is also a Weavers Way sign here.

    Walk through this farm yard with the big metal barn on your right and continue along the drive to a house which has a pond on the right. Where the drive turns right, you walk straight ahead through a little wooded area which open out onto a wide track with hedges either side (signed for Weavers Way). Continue along here, reaching a wood on your right-hand side called Allotment Plantation, and the path brings you out onto another lane.

12. Turn right here and walk a very short distance until you see a Weavers Way sign on the right-hand side of the road but pointing to the woodland on the left. Take this path through the woodland, following the track all the way to the lake at Felbrigg Hall.

13. Just before the lake, turn left, walking through the woodland and keeping the lake on your right. Continue to follow the path until you reach the gate. Go through this gate and follow the path bearing right until you reach a large oak tree and a couple of National Trust signs pointing to the way ahead. Here the path forks. Take the right-hand fork along a well-trodden path down towards a gate and a bridge which

crosses the edge of the reed-covered lake. You have no option but to follow this path all the way to another gate.

14. However, half way along here by a short stretch of a board walk, is a Sessile Oak tree which is thought to be about 500 years old and 9 meters in circumference. (You can walk through the gate here and head up towards the Hall should you wish).

15. Continue past the oak tree until you reach a gate. Once through the gate, bear right until you reach a wrought iron gate and cattle grid to Felbrigg Hall. As you walk along this short path you will see a different side to Felbrigg Hall. Follow the path back to the car park keeping the Hall on your left.

Walk 11. Oxburgh and Gooderstone walk (4.9 miles)

Oxburgh Hall, just south of Swaffham, is a magnificent and impressive moated Tudor gatehouse dating back to 1482. It was built by Sir Edmund Bedingfeld and has been in the same family for all that time, but is now managed by the National Trust. The interior is steeped in history.

This house is not on the grand scale of some of the other Norfolk stately homes such as Houghton Hall and Holkham, but has a very intimate feel about it. One of the bedrooms has a four-poster bed in which Henry VII slept, and you can also see the very beautiful and intricate needlework on display that was sewn by Anne, Queen of Scots and Bess of Hardwick.

The Priest's Hole is another attraction – built to house the resident priest of the time. As the Bedingfeld's were catholic, they sometimes housed a priest to celebrate mass, but in the post-reformation era it was illegal to practice Catholicism so they had to make sure the priest was never seen. The Priest would disappear into the hole if the house was searched by the authorities. You can climb into it if you are nimble and small enough!

The church of St John the Evangelist, just next door to Oxburgh Hall, is now a stunning but important part ruin/part working chapel. In 1948 the tower toppled and collapsed into the church. However, the 16th Century Bedingfeld Chapel remained untouched and is still in use today. It's worth going into the chapel where you'll see some of the finest terracotta tombs in the UK. It's beautiful inside.

ROUTE DIRECTIONS

Map Details: OS Explorer 236

Postcode: PE33 9PS. This postcode takes you to Oxborough village (spelt differently to Oxburgh Hall)

Grading: Easy, with one stile (OK for dogs)

What to expect: the ruins of St John's Church at the beginning of the walk, quiet country lanes, farmland and tracks, Gooderstone village and Oxburgh Hall (if you wish to visit this after or before your walk)

Dog friendly: Yes, but there is a bit of road walking near and in Gooderstone village. Dogs are allowed in the gardens and woodlands of Oxburgh Hall

Length: 4.8 miles

Time: 1 ¾ hours

Start Location: St John's Church where road side parking is available (or the pub if you are stopping afterwards)

Facilities: The Bedingfeld Arms and Oxburgh Hall

Entry Cost: National Trust cost for Oxburgh Hall and car park. No charge for parking in the village around St John's Church

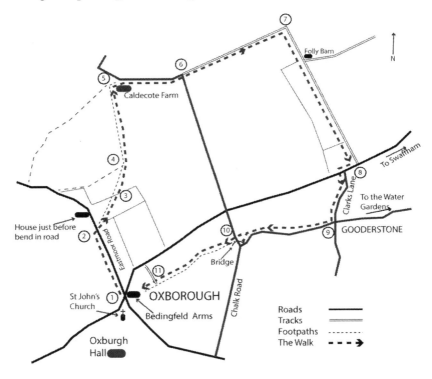

1. With your back to the ruins of St John's church, walk over the main road to Eastmore Road. Follow this straight lane into open countryside.

2. Just before you reach a house and a bend in the road, look out for a footpath sign pointing right (the sign is on the left-

hand verge). Walk through this field diagonally until you reach the hedge in front of you.

3. Turn right and almost immediately you'll see a gap in the hedge with the waymarker. Walk through the hedge and continue across the next field diagonally. These are permissive paths.

4. Once at the end of this field turn left and follow the track all the way until you reach a farm building and a tarmac lane. This is called Caldecote Farm.

5. Continue straight ahead along this road for short while until it bends sharply round to the right. Do NOT go right, (unless you want a shorter walk). Carry straight on along a wide farm track with hedgerows on either side.

6. Walk along the track until the hedge stops and becomes open fields with the post and wire fence. Turn right here and continue along the slightly narrower track, passing Folly Barn on your left, until you reach the tarmac lane.

7. Turn right onto the lane and then take the first left, Clarks Lane. Follow this lane all the way into Gooderstone village.

8. At the T junction in the village, turn right, and follow the road all the way out of the village. Once out of the village, you will come to a sharp right-hand bend, walking past Chalk Road on your left. Continue to walk over the small bridge. Just after the bridge is a small footpath sign and the stile on the left.

9. Take this path, heading across a grassy field until you reach a hedge at the far right-hand corner. Walk through the gap in this hedge and continue along the side of the field.

10. Once you reach the end of this field, cross straight over the gravel drive (this drive goes to the fishing lakes) and head along the narrow path for a short distance (beech hedge on the right this time) until you reach a stile in the hedge. This path takes you along the back of some houses and eventually brings you out onto a road where you turn left and you'll see The Bedingfeld Arms ahead and where you started your walk.

Walk 12. Bircham Windmill (5.1 miles)

B ircham Windmill was built in 1846 and has now been completely restored to how it would have looked over 100 years ago. During the 19th century there were over 300 working windmills, but this one is now the only working windmill in the area which is open to the public, **but only from April to September**. I have put this walk in the book due to the heritage of the windmill.

It's still a magnificent site to walk past in the winter, but you could visit it in the summer months and see it working, climb the five floors up to the fan and see the machinery in operation. It still has the original coal fired oven, flour is still milled and bread is still baked in the original bakery.

ROUTE DIRECTIONS

Map Details: OS Explorer 250

Postcode: PE31 6RJ

Grading: Easy

What to expect: One of the few working windmills in the UK, walking along a stretch of the historic Peddars Way and very peaceful grassy tracks.

Dog friendly: Yes, for the walk, *but they are **not** permitted into the tearooms, bakery or windmill.* There is a little stretch of road walking past the windmill and down a quiet lane. They are allowed into the garden and grounds of the windmill

Length: 5.1 miles

Time: 2 hours

Start Location: In the winter months you can park in the village of Bircham, opposite the pub, or there is a small layby, also opposite the pub. In the summer months you can park at Bircham Windmill car park (free) and start the walk from the windmill.

Facilities: WC, Bircham Windmill café and viewing in the summer months, or the The King's Head pub in Bircham all year round.

Entry Cost: Charge for the windmill, but free entry into the Bakery, tea rooms and gift shop **(open April-September).** Free car parking in both Bircham and Bircham Windmill.

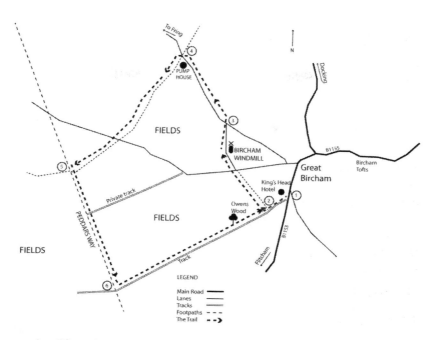

1. If you're starting from the village of Bircham, there are a
    few places to park. There is a small layby almost opposite
    the pub, or there is space by Bircham Stores (also opposite
    the pub). If you are starting from the windmill in the
    summer months, you park in the designated car park and
    start this walk from the windmill (point 3).

    From Bircham village head south for a very short distance
    walking away from the pub. You will then see a track on the
    right-hand side of the road with houses either side. Take this
    track and walk straight ahead along the obvious path.

2. A short distance along here (and before the track bears
    slightly round to the right) the hedge opens up into fields
    with a large grassy track on the right. Turn right here and
    walk in the direction of the windmill. The grass track
    becomes a bit narrower and is surrounded either side by
    hedgerows. You'll eventually reach a quiet lane. Cross

71

straight over here and head towards the windmill which you'll easily see. Continue along this lane (passing the windmill on your right) until you reach the T Junction (and continue the walk from No 4 below).

If you park at the windmill in the summer months, this is where you start. Turn right out of the car park and walk along the quiet narrow lane to the T Junction.

3.   At the T Junction, turn left and walk along the lane down the hill enjoying the views over the countryside.

4.   At the pump house (at the bottom of the hill and which is very obvious to see - behind metal gates), take a grass farm track on the left and walk along this path in a westerly direction. Continue along the path, crossing over a tarmac lane until you reach a grass T junction which is the Peddars Way.

5.   Turn left and walk along the Peddars Way for one mile. Continue south until you reach a crossroads of grassy farm tracks. At this point you should see a wooden sign on the left pointing to the King's Arms and Bircham Village Stores.

6.   Take this left-hand track heading all the way back towards Bircham. **If you parked in Bircham, continue along this track back to the village**.

If you parked at the windmill, continue with the directions below.

In just over a mile you'll pass Owens Wood. Look out for a track on your left. This is fairly obvious and has a hedge on the right (this is before you reach the village of Bircham). Once you've turned left along the track, you'll also see some houses and barn conversions in the distance on the right-hand side. Continue along this path, cross over another lane where you'll see the windmill ahead of you. Walk back to the car park.

Walk 13. Horsey Windpump (5 miles)

Horsey Windpump (as opposed to a windmill) is an iconic sight along the bumpy coastal road at Horsey and is the epitome of the Norfolk Broads. It's surrounded by views of water meadows, dykes and the sand dunes in the distance. This is somewhere you get drawn into and just want to stop and visit, which I why I love this walk. This walk also offers you the chance to see the seals and their seal pups during the winter months along Horsey beach (usually from November to January/February).

Horsey Windpump was built in 1912 on 18th century foundations and played a huge part in draining the surrounding fields and pumping the water into the river. In the 1900's Horsey was pretty much an island surrounded by marshes with one road in and out of the village, and was often flooded for most of the year.

Horsey Windpump is managed by the National Trust. You can pay to climb the top of the mill which will give you spectacular views over the Broadland landscape and entry will also enable you to see the cogs that turn the sails.

The Windpump has had its fair share of disasters. In March 1895 the cap blew off into the road. In 1912 work started on taking it down, brick by brick, as it was in a dangerous condition. In July 1943 it was struck by lightning. In the gales of 1987, the fantail blew off and the cap was severely damaged.

After a 3-year restoration project, in 2019 the sails on Horsey Windpump started to turn once again after 76 years!

ROUTE DIRECTIONS

Map Details: OS Explorer OL40

Postcode: NR29 4EF

Grading: Easy walking, flat, but could be muddy in the winter months. One stile (not good for big dogs) but is adjacent to a metal gate which can be opened

What to expect: Horsey Mere, Horsey beach, the seals in the winter months (Nov-Feb), reed beds, meadows, dykes, farmland, WWII pill box, the ruin of Brograve Drainage Mill, the National Trust Horsey Windpump

Dog friendly: Possibly, *but* there may be cattle in the water meadows at the beginning, and if you want to see the seals it's best to go without them. You would also need a keep them on a lead for a lot of the walk so that they are under control with the wildlife in the reed beds etc. There is also a stile which a large dog won't get through, but there is a metal gate adjacent to the stile

Length: 5 miles

Time: 2 ½ hours without a stop to see the seals in the winter

Start Location: National Trust Horsey Windpump car park – a charge applies

Facilities: NT shop and tea room, WC, pub in the village and Poppyland Tea room in Horsey

Entry Cost: National Trust charge for car park and entry to climb Horsey Windpump.

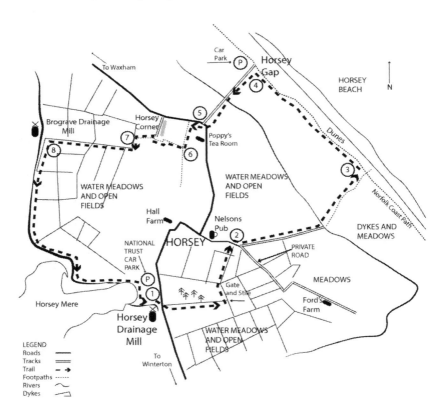

1. Park in the National Trust Car Park at Horsey Windpump where you'll find WC's and a small tea room. Cross over the main road and enter through the gate into a water meadow to then follow the fairly well-trodden track with a dyke on one side and open fields on the other side. Follow this track (with a small copse on your left) until you reach a large dyke and can go no further. Turn left here, climbing over the style (there is also a metal gate here) and continue along the farm track, with dykes on your right, until you reach a tarmacked road.

2. At the tarmac road, turn right. A short distance from here, the road forks. Take the left-hand fork, heading towards the sea, passing a metal barrier gate. Walk along this path with reed beds and meadows on either side, until you reach the dunes.

3. Here you can visit the viewing platform for the seals if you're walking in the winter months. This path that you have just reached is part of the Norfolk Coast Path.
Turn left here and continue until you reach the Horsey Gap car park. You could walk along the beach as an alternative.

4. Once at Horsey Gap car park, turn left and follow the track away from the beach until you meet the main road. (You'll see the Poppyland Tearooms on the corner).

5. Turn right on the main road and walk a short distance of about 100 meters along here until you see a footpath sign to the left pointing you to walk through the field. Follow the

path along the field, keeping a small dyke on your left, until you reach a hedge.

6. Turn right here towards a small cluster of houses and this will bring you out onto a small quiet lane. Turn right and them almost immediately turn left to walk along another signed footpath, keeping the house on your left. Walk out towards open land.

7. Once you reach a dyke, cross over the wooden footbridge and head towards the old relic of Brograve Drainage Mill. A great opportunity here to take some wonderful photos of this Mill.

8. Once at the Mill, turn left and follow the path all the way, walking alongside the river to eventually arrive at Horsey Mere and the National Trust car park and Windpump.

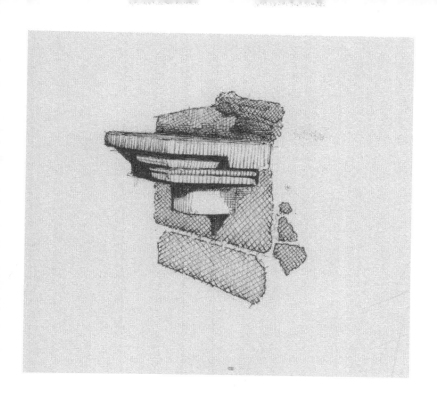

79

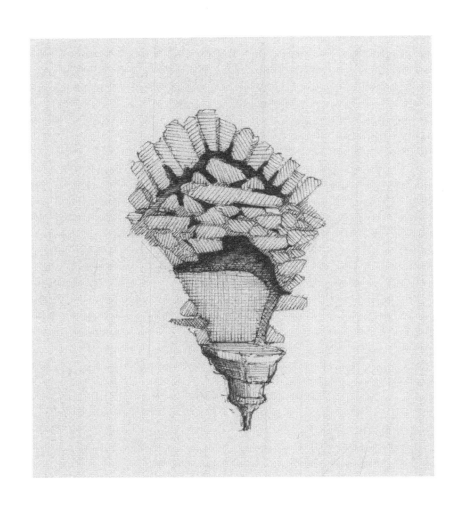

Walk 14. Bawsey Ruin (5.6 miles)

Bawsey ruin is the remains of St James Church. Although the ruin now stands in isolation, it once stood proudly in the middle of the busy village of Bawsey St James. There are no signs left to show streets or houses, but pottery has been found over the years on this site dating back to the Iron Age.

The village was destroyed in the 16th Century by the landowner to make way for more grazing land for his sheep, and the only thing that wasn't demolished was the church, although it did fall into disrepair. Like many of the ruins in Norfolk, it was built in 1109, during the Norman period.

This walk also takes you along the edge of Roydon Common and through Grimston Warren. Grimston Warren was afforested in the 1960's but in 1999 the Norfolk Wildlife Trust began a decade long conservation plan on Roydon Common, and in 2004 they started on

Grimston Warren. Both the Common and the Warren now look spectacular and in very good shape. Cattle and Dartmoor ponies are used to keep the heath in good shape and you may well come across them during this walk.

ROUTE DIRECTIONS

Map Details: OS Explorer 250

Postcode: PE32 1EU

Grading: Easy walking

What to expect: Ancient ruins of St James church, open countryside and farmland, tracks and paths, common land, heathland, Dartmoor ponies and cattle. It can be a little noisy near the beginning of the walk due to the busy A148 but you'll soon experience peace once you walk towards Grimston Warren

Dog friendly: Yes, *but please keep them on a lead through the Warren as rare heathland species breed here, and you may come across the ponies or cattle.* Part of this walk is also working farmland so please respect the countryside by closing gates and keeping dogs under control

Length: 5.6 miles

Time: 2 hours

Start Location: Church Farm, Bawsey, PE32 1EU. This is a little rural lane turning off the B1145 and can be difficult to spot if going too fast!

Facilities: None

Entry Cost: None

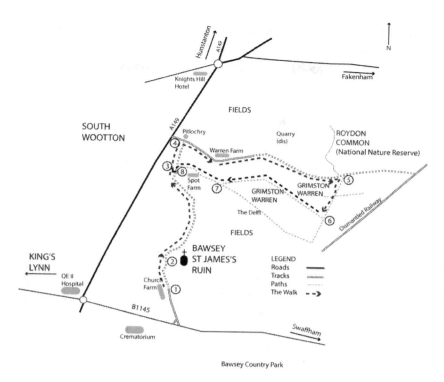

Bawsey Country Park

1. Park at Church Farm on the wide grass verge opposite the farm and head along the track keeping the farm buildings on your left. This wide track takes you all the way to Bawsey church ruin with open fields on either side. Once at the ruin you can take a bit of time to walk around it and admire the view across the countryside.

2. To continue the walk, turn right out of the ruins and follow this winding farm track all the way until you reach a farm track junction (there is also a house and farm buildings on the right-hand side – Spot Farm).

3. Carry on straight ahead until you reach a tarmac road and a house in front of you called Pitlochry.

4. Turn right here, walking along the road and through a bit of woodland. You'll pass a holiday accommodation on your left. The road soon turns into a track with open fields on either side. You'll pass a strange tall brick structure on your left in the middle of a field, and you eventually reach Roydon Common on your left and Grimston Warren on your right. You'll know this because the Commons are fenced and you're surrounded by heather. Continue to walk along the sandy track, passing a gate on your left which goes into Roydon Common.

5. Continue on a little bit further until you come across the entrance to Grimston Warren on your right. You'll easily see this as there are about 3 metal gates and an information board about Grimston Warren. Go through the gate and continue to walk along the track until you reach a crossroads of paths. Continue straight ahead in the same direction until the path bears round to the right as well as a slightly narrower path going straight on.

6. Follow the path around to the right crossing through the heathland, heather on either side, until you start to walk down a slight incline and reach the edge of the common with a metal gate in front of you. Here you may see the Dartmoor ponies.

7. Walk through the gate and join the track. Walk through another gate and pass Spot Farm on your left-hand side.

8. Join the track that you came up on and turn left to walk all the way back to Bawsey ruin and Church Farm where you left your car.

Walk 15. 3 possible walks to Ludham Bridge, St Benet's Abbey, Toad Hole Museum and the How Hill Estate

St Benet's Abbey was one of Norfolk's first monasteries and is of huge importance as it's the only monastery not to be dissolved by Henry VIII. Although it wasn't dissolved, the Abbot was made Bishop of Norwich, but only on condition that he gave properties to the Crown. The Bishop of Norwich is still connected to St Benet's Abbey; every year on the first Sunday in August he conducts an open-air service.

The ruin is an odd one in that it has an old mill right in the middle of the gatehouse. The mill has nothing to do with the abbey but was built in the 1720's to crush oil seed and they used the gatehouse as a support!

The other structure you'll notice in the surrounds of the Abbey is a large wooden cross made from oak and was commissioned in 1987 from the Sandringham Estate. It's placed where the high alter of the Abbey would have been.

These Ludham walks contain three possible trails of varying length, all starting in the village of Ludham and visiting St Benet's Abbey (if you choose) and/or the tiny Toad Hole museum on the How Hill Estate and walking amongst the wonderful Broads landscape of rivers and reedbeds.

5.3 mile circular walk to St Benet's Abbey and Ludham Bridge

ROUTE DIRECTIONS

Map Details: OS Explorer OL40

Postcode: NR29 5QQ

Grading: Easy

What to expect: Historic Ludham Hall (and the chapel which you can just make out attached to the side of the Hall (the Hall is of Jacobean origin and belonged to the Bishops of Norwich), a bit of road walking, St Benet's Abbey, Broads footpath and reed beds along the River Bure to Ludham Bridge, quiet lanes, Ludham village with splendid church. *Although these walks look like you walk alongside the River Bure and Ant, the path is actually below the river bank so you won't see the typical Broads boats on this walk. But the paths do meanders alongside smaller parallel side channels and you are still very much in amongst the reed beds and dykes of typical Broads landscape*

Dog friendly: Yes, although there is quite a lot of road walking

Length: 5.3 miles

Time: Approx 2 hours

Start Location: The church in Ludham

Facilities: Café, pub, local shop

Entry Cost: Free parking in the village of Ludham and free entry to the surrounds of St Benet's Abbey

LUDHAM TO ST BENET'S ABBEY MAP - 5.3 MILE WALK

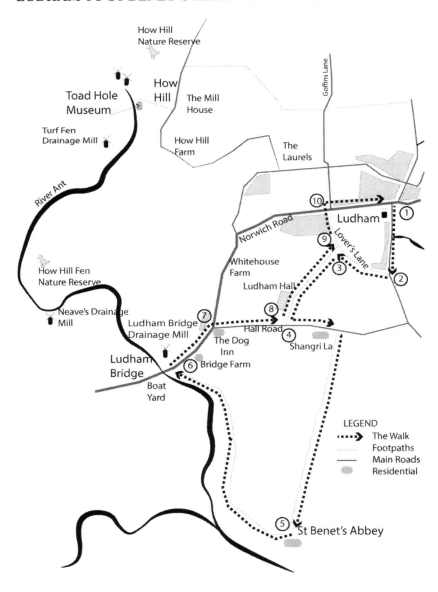

1. With the church on your right and facing away from the pub and sharp corner of the main road, head down the hill along the quiet Staithe Road. Pass a staithe on your left and continue along this road until you reach Lover's Lane on your right (opposite a caravan park).

2. Turn right along this tarmac dead-end road. This becomes a grassy track surrounded by open fields. Continue along this track until you reach a junction in the tracks.

3. Turn left along here keeping the tall hedge on your right and open fields on your left. You'll see farm buildings in the distance. Head towards Ludham Hall. Walk through Ludham Hall yard, noticing the lovely barns on your left and the pretty house on your right. Continue through the farm, walking down the slight incline until you reach Hall Lane.

4. Turn left along here for a short distance. Take the first right (signposted to St Benet's Abbey). Pass a farm and just continue along this tarmac track until you reach St Benet's Abbey.

   Once at St Benet's Abbey, enjoy some time to wander around the ruins.

5. Walk away from St Benet's Abbey following the footpath which takes you all the way along the River Bure to eventually arrive at Ludham Bridge.

6. Turn right here and walk along the pavement of the busy road for about 5 minutes.

7. Take the first right, signposted to Hall Common and continue along this lane until you reach Ludham Hall again.

8. Turn left into Ludham Hall and retrace your steps until you reach the junction in the fields.

9. Here you turn left and walk towards the village.

10. Once at the main road, turn right and continue to walk into Ludham village and returning to the church and where you parked your car.

6.3 mile walk to Ludham Bridge, Toad Hole and How Hill

Toad Hole Cottage, on the How Hill Estate, is now a tiny museum, but well worth a visit if you're going to go for a walk here. It's a tiny thatched two-bedroom cottage that housed a whole family in the Victorian times. Situated right on the River Ant, it was used by the Marshmen who were eel catchers. It's an interesting bit of history showcasing lots of tools and food preservation techniques that were used when it was inhabited. It's amazing to think how this small cottage slept a whole family.

ROUTE DIRECTIONS

Map Details: OS Explorer OL40

Postcode: NR29 5QQ

Grading: Easy

What to expect: A mixture of scenery from open fields to Broads landscapes, reed beds and grazing marshes. Historic Ludham Hall (and the chapel which you can just make out attached to the side of the Hall (the Hall is of Jacobean origin and belonged to the Bishops of Norwich), a bit of road walking along quiet lanes, Broads footpath and swathes of reed beds along the River Ant to How Hill, Toad Hole museum (**open from April and October and free entry**) picturesque How Hill House, drainage mills, Ludham village with splendid church

Dog friendly: Not really as quite a bit of road walking

Length: 6.3 miles

Time: Approx 2.5 hours

Start Location: The church in Ludham

Facilities: Café, pub, local shop in the village. Tea Room at How Hill (**open May to September on Saturdays and Sundays and every day during summer school holidays**)

Entry Cost: Free parking in the village of Ludham and free to visit Toad Hall Museum

LUDHAM TO HOW HILL AND TOAD HOLE COTTAGE - 6.3 MILE WALK

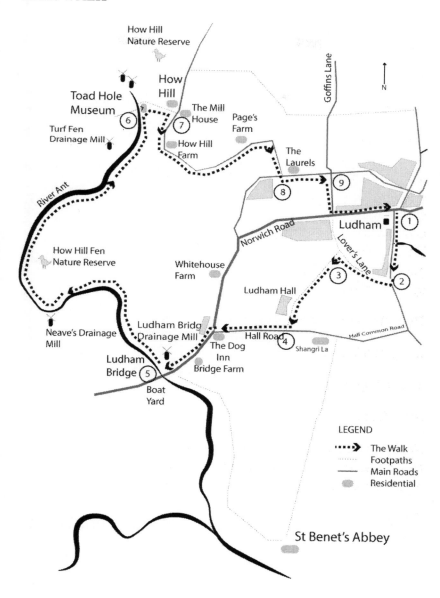

1. With the church on your right and facing away from the pub and sharp corner of the main road, head down the hill along the quiet Staithe Road. Pass a staithe on your left and continue along this road until you reach Lover's Lane on your right (opposite a caravan park).

2. Turn right along this tarmac dead-end road. This becomes a grassy track surrounded by open fields. Continue along this track until you reach a junction in the tracks.

3. Turn left along here, following the track and keeping the tall hedge on your right and open field on your left. You'll see farm buildings in the distance. Head towards Ludham Hall. Walk through the Ludham Hall yard, noticing the lovely barns on your left and the pretty house on your right. Continue through the farm, walking down the slight incline until you reach Hall Lane.

4. At Hall Lane, turn right and continue along here until you reach a T junction with a thatched cottage in front of you. Turn left and continue along the busy road for approximately 5 minutes until you reach Ludham Bridge (you will soon be in the peace and quiet!).

5. Walk to Ludham Bridge, turn right and follow the path alongside the river (river on your left). You'll walk past the derelict Ludham Bridge Drainage Mill on your right. Continue along the path with the raised bank on your left and reed beds and grazing marshes on your right. Soon, in the distance you'll see the very picturesque thatched How Hill resplendent on the hill. Eventually you find yourself walking towards a copse of trees. When you reach here, follow the path around to the left (very obvious) and walk parallel with the dyke heading towards How Hill and the moorings. On your right you'll see the beautifully kept

gardens of How Hill. Walk along the moorings which are opposite Turf Fen Drainage Mill.

6. Towards the far end of the moorings you'll notice a wooden bridge to the right. Take this and visit Toad Hole Cottage Museum. Once you've visited the tiny cottage, turn right out of the little shop and follow a rough track up an incline to How Hill and out onto the lane. Note the Olympic Oak commemoration just before you reach the lane on the left.

7. Once at the lane (Mill House is opposite you), turn right and head down the hill to walk along the quiet and pretty lane, passing Page's Farm. Continue to follow the road, walking around a sharp right-hand bend until you reach a T junction.

8. Turn left here (signposted to Catfield and Potter Heigham).

9. At the next staggered cross roads, take the right turn and continue along here until you reach the main road. Turn left, and walk along the pavement all the way back to the village of Ludham and returning to the church and your car.

8.35 miles to St Benet's Abbey, Ludham Bridge, Toad Hole

How Hill, a thatched Edwardian manor house, sits on one of the highest point in the Broads district. At the turn of the century Edward Boardman purchased 800 acres of land bordering the River Ant. The most striking feature was a hillock of glacial sand and gravel 50 feet above sea level, and this is where he decided he'd build his thatched house. You'll see it from quite a distance.

In 1966, after his death, the estate was split and Norfolk County Council Education Department bought the house as well as some of the marshes, woodland and gardens. In 1984, the How Hill Trust was set up and now provides Environmental Education in the form of residential field courses and day visits for school children and young people.

This walk joins both of the above two walks which include the historic St Benet's Abbey and Toad Hole.

ROUTE DIRECTIONS

Map Details: OS Explorer OL40

Postcode: NR29 5QQ

Grading: Easy

What to expect: The same as the other 2 walks mentioned

Dog friendly: Not really as there is quite a lot of road walking

Length: 8.3 miles

Time: Approx 4 hours

Start Location: The church in Ludham

Facilities: Café, pub, local shop in the village. Tea Room at How Hill (**open May to September on Saturdays and Sundays and every day during summer school holidays**)

Entry Cost: Free parking in the village of Ludham and free to visit Toad Hall Museum

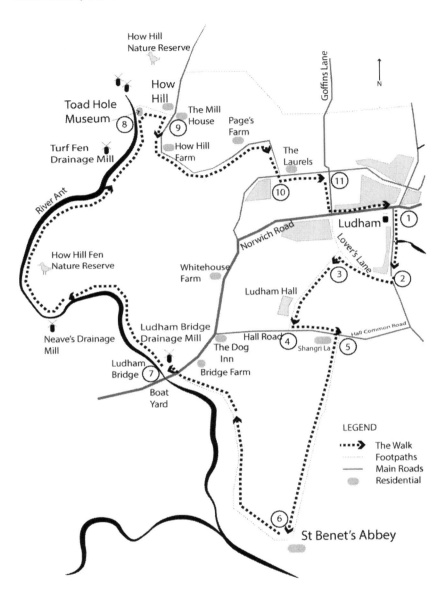

1. With the church on your right and facing away from the pub and sharp corner of the main road, head down the hill along the quiet Staithe Road. Pass a staithe on your left and continue along this road until you reach Lover's Lane on your right (opposite a caravan park).

2. Turn right along this tarmac dead-end road. This becomes a grassy track surrounded by open fields. Continue along this track until you reach a junction in the tracks.

3. Turn left along here, following the track and keeping the tall hedge on your right and open field on your left. You'll see farm buildings in the distance. Head towards Ludham Hall. Walk through the Ludham Hall yard, noticing the lovely barns on your left and the pretty house on your right. Continue through the farm, walking down the slight incline until you reach Hall Lane.

4. Turn left along here for a short distance.

5. Take the first right (signposted to St Benet's Abbey). Pass a farm and just continue along this tarmac track until you reach St Benet's Abbey.

6. Once at St Benet's Abbey, enjoy some time to wander around the ruins. Walk away from St Benet's Abbey following the footpath which takes you all the way along the River Ant to the main road.

7. Turn left and eventually arrive at Ludham Bridge. Turn right and follow the path alongside the river. You'll walk past the derelict Ludham Bridge Drainage Mill on your right. Continue along the path with the raised bank on your left and reed beds and grazing marshes on your right. Soon, in the distance you'll see the very picturesque thatched How

Hill resplendent on the hill. Eventually you find yourself walking towards a copse of trees. When you reach here, follow the path around to the left (very obvious) and walk parallel with the dyke heading towards How Hill and the moorings. On your right you'll see the beautifully kept gardens of How Hill. Walk along the moorings which are opposite Turf Fen Drainage Mill.

8. Towards the far end of the moorings you'll notice a wooden bridge to the right. Take this and visit Toad Hole Cottage Museum. Once you've visited the tiny cottage, turn right out of the little shop and follow a rough track up an incline to How Hill and out onto the lane. Note the Olympic Oak commemoration just before you reach the lane on the left.

9. Once at the lane (Mill House is opposite), turn right and head down the hill to walk along the quiet and pretty lane, passing Page's Farm. Continue to follow the road, walking around a sharp right-hand bend until you reach a T junction.

10. Turn left here (signposted to Catfield and Potter Heigham).

11. At the next staggered cross roads, take the right turn and continue along here until you reach the main road. Turn left, and walk along the pavement all the way back to the village of Ludham and returning to the church.

Walk 16. Holkham Hall (6-7 miles)

Holkham Hall is probably one of the most impressive stately homes in Norfolk with vast grounds that you can explore. It is an 18th century Palladian mansion which is privately owned by the Coke family (pronounced Cook, and who also own Castle Acre Priory and the Castle at Castle Acre).

Work on Holkham Hall started in 1734, took 30 years to build and was designed by the well-known architect, William Kent, protégé to Lord Burlington. The interior rooms are incredibly opulent and house many treasures. You'll also find a chapel in the house.

The grounds are also beautiful, with miles of rolling countryside where you will probably be lucky enough to see the fallow deer. If you love gardens, it would be worth paying to see the walled garden at the same time. Holkham Hall is a real treat to visit.

This particular walk is a wonderful amble around the parkland, as well as giving you the opportunity to visit the Hall, courtyard café for refreshments, and, if you like gardening, you can also walk to the fantastic walled garden. There is a charge for visiting the house and garden.

ROUTE DIRECTIONS

Map Details: OS Explorer 251

Postcode: NR23 1RG

Grading: Easy

What to expect: Grand Palladian Hall, Courtyard café, Field to Fork museum (£), deer, obelisk, ancient ice house, woodlands, lake, immaculate walled garden (£), family church, courtyard café. **Be aware though, that the house is only open on Sunday's, Monday's and Thursday's during the summer months. The park, café and shop are open all year round (depending on weather) apart from Christmas Day**

Dog friendly: Yes, under control as there are roaming deer

Length: 6-7 miles

Time: 3 hours or all day depending on what you choose to do. You can eat in the Courtyard Café, visit the impressive walled garden and the interior or the Hall and walk around the parkland

Start Location: Park in Lady Anne's Drive, (pay and display machine – cards can be used).) or the free car park in Holkham village which is just up the private road from The Victoria Inn. Start from The Victoria Inn, Park Road, Holkham

Facilities: Courtyard café, WC

Entry Cost: Car parking charges and fee to enter the house and walled garden.

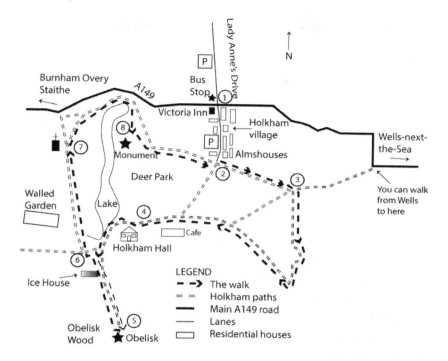

1. Start at The Victoria Inn on the main A149 coastal road (right by the bus stop on the map) or park at the car park in St Lady Anne's Drive (opposite The Victoria Inn), and head inland towards Holkham Hall, walking past the worker's cottages and on towards the arched gateway.

2. Once through the gateway, take an immediate left and enjoy the woodland walk, passing through one metal gate with two rather interesting latches. This is a lovely quiet stretch through pleasant woodland.

3. At the obvious junction, turn slightly right and walk over the cattle grid into beautiful parkland. Follow this path, walking over another cattle grid until you reach the Holkham Hall car

park and on towards the Hall. Once here you can then visit the Courtyard café for refreshments. There is also a WC here!

4. Walk out of the courtyard and turn left, passing the front of the house. Bear left here (with the lake on your right) and this is where you continue up the hill, passing an amazingly shaped historic ice house on your right, and on to the obelisk, which is just over another cattle grid. The ice house is one of the oldest buildings (other than the church) within Holkham Park, built around 1730. Note: almost opposite the ice house, on your left-hand side, is a small path between some lovely oak trees. If you walk along there, you'll discover a bench and a bronze sculpture of the previous Lord Leicester, sitting with his spaniel and admiring Holkham Hall from a distance – this gives you a very good view of the house.

5. The walk up to the obelisk adds another one mile to the walk (approximately). The obelisk was the first work built in the Park around 1720, apparently to signal the intention of the 1st Earl to build a grand hall.

6. If you don't walk to the obelisk, turn right at the end of the

lake and follow the path right on the edge of the lake until you reach a fence (which directs you to the walled garden ahead). If you like gardens, this is one worth visiting but is an extra cost. Once at the fence, turn right and walk through the open field towards the church. The Church of St Withburga dates back to the 13th Century.

7. Once at the church, bear right (don't carry on straight) and continue into the woodlands and towards the lake. Follow the track all the way around the end of the lake until you reach a junction with a path to the right and straight on.

8. Turn right for a short distance until you see the Monument which is a Corinthian column, and then continue left, following the path all the way back to the archway and Alms Houses at the entrance to Holkham Hall. Retrace your steps back to The Victoria Inn, the bus stop or car park.

Walk 17. Castle Acre Priory (6 miles)

Castle Acre Priory is a spectacular ruin and one of the largest and most impressive monastic ruins in England. It's also one of the best-preserved priory ruins in the UK.

Founded in 1089, it was originally situated within the castle ruins which are at the other end of the village. Due to the inconvenience, it was then moved to the present location about a year after the castle was built.

The Priory, along with many others in Norfolk, was dissolved by Henry VIII in 1537. Eventually, the Priory was passed to the Coke family who own Holkham Hall, and both Castle Acre Priory and Castle Acre Castle are still owned by the Coke's. It is now managed by English Heritage. The Priory appears large from the outside, but, if you have the time, I would suggest you pay to go into the interior. It's even more impressive from the inside than it is from the outside.

This Castle Acre Circular Walk is an easy and incredibly varied stroll alongside the picturesque River Nar (a lovely chalk stream), and the flood meadows, taking in part of the Nar Valley Way trail, and continuing on through attractive woodland and out onto open fields, along hedgerows full of wildlife. You'll also have wonderful views across the countryside, and finally finish, walking past the ancient ruins of Castle Acre Priory. Once in the village, you can have a well-deserved drink/lunch/tea in the local pub, The Ostrich Inn, or at the tea rooms.

ROUTE DIRECTIONS

Map Details: OS Explorer 236

Postcode: PE32 2AE

Grading: Easy with a slight incline up to the fields (points 5 & 6 on the map)

What to expect: Clear chalk stream of the River Nar, woodland, open fields, Castle Acre Priory, flint stone village of Castle Acre

Dog friendly: Yes

Length: 6 miles

Time: 2.5 hours

Start Location: You can park in the village opposite The Ostrich Pub and around the Bailey Gate and Green. Free parking

Facilities: pub and tea room in the village

Entry Cost: A charge to visit the Priory

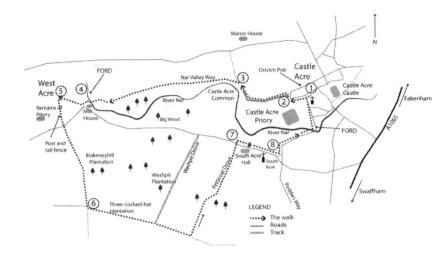

1. Start by walking away from the village with the church on your left and the pub on your right and head along the road towards The Priory (signposted) with the remains of the flintstone wall on your left.

2. Follow the road round to the right (with the Priory on your left). At the next corner take the track to the left (all very well signposted as the circular walk (blue) and at this point The Nar Valley Way as well, (pink)). Follow this track down to the River Nar where you come across a wooden kissing.

3. Turn left to walk alongside the River Nar, continuing along the flood meadow to the start of an undulating woodland path which eventually brings you to a board walk, two footbridges, an attractive imposing mill house, and a short way after that, a tarmac road. All of this stretch is very obvious to follow, the river and paths through the wood are well trodden.

4. Once you reach the tarmac road, it's worth just turning righ to the ford and standing on the bridge over the River Nar and admiring the beautiful river. Look to see if you can see any trout swimming along in the clear chalk stream, or just while a way a few minutes relaxing at the slow pace of life. To continue on your walk, retrace your steps from the ford up the slight incline to the grass car park on the right. Turn right here and head along a short stretch of heathland.

5. A short way along this heathland bear left along a narrow footpath (almost coming back on yourself). This path has a hedge on the right with a view of West Acre Priory, and a post and wire fence on the left-hand side. At the end of this track you'll reach a tarmac road. Cross straight and continue up the hill along a track running between fields on either side. Continue on up past a wood on your left (but at this

stage do turn around and admire the fantastic view of the remoteness of Norfolk). Carry on straight past the wood, continuing up the hill until you reach the end of the field.

6. Turn left here and stroll along the well-worn tracks with the hedge on your left and open countryside on both sides of you (there are signs all the way along this walk, you can't go wrong!). From here, just follow the signs, walking along the farm tracks that eventually bring you back down to another tarmac road with a wonderful beech hedge.

7. From here, turn right, walk along the pleasant country lane, passing South Acre Church as well as a few very pretty houses.

8. Take the first left-hand fork before a sharp corner. This is a very quiet lane, and you quickly get a chance to have spectacular views over the ruins of Castle Acre Priory This road brings you to another ford.
    Walk over the bridge and again, just take time to admire the view of Castle Acre Priory from this standpoint. If you wish, you could deviate and take a walk around the exterior of the Priory, but if you just want to get back to the village, follow the road up the hill and this will bring you back to the church and finally the village!

If you wanted to take some time to see the Castle ruins, all you need to do is walk straight through the village, passing the pub on your left and at the sharp left-hand corner is a small lane which will take you to the ruins and wonderful views over the surrounding countryside.

111

Walk 18. Castle Rising (7 miles)

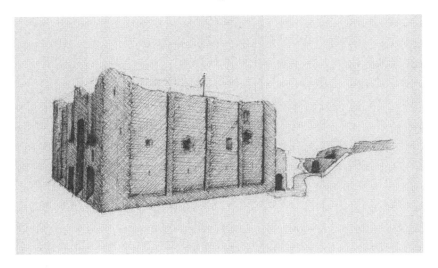

Castle Rising Castle is a magnificent and opposing structure built in the 12th century (Norman times) and sits on the west coast of Norfolk with views out to The Wash. It's one of the most important well-known keeps in all of England and is now managed by English Heritage.

It's weathered the years very well and still looks quite intact. It was built by William d'Albini for his new wife, but I don't believe he ever built it for the purpose of defending himself, so it was much more a residence than an actual Castle. The most famous inhabitant of Castle Rising Castle was Queen Isabella, widow of Edward III. It's alleged that she murdered her husband and consequently used the Castle as her main residence thereafter.

It's thought that this Castle was modelled on Norwich Castle which is definitely very similar in appearance. If you've got the time, it's worth paying the entrance fee and visiting the ruins because there are some very well-preserved rooms, wonderful stone steps, narrow passages and walkways with arrow slits in the walls giving amazing views towards The Wash.

ROUTE DIRECTIONS

Map Details: OS Explorer 236

Postcode: PE31 6AG

Grading: Easy, but could be muddy in the winter months. 4 stiles

What to expect: The Castle is **closed during the winter months** but this walk starts from the car park in the village. Castle Rising Castle (when open is worth the visit), the pretty flintstone village, woodland and the River Babingley, meadows, farm tracks and open countryside. *There is a bit of road walking (one short 4 min walk along the verge of the busy main A148 which is a little unpleasant but if you keep back from the road, it's OK) and crossing over a couple of busy roads.*

Dog friendly: No

Length: 6 miles

Time: 2 ¼ hours

Start Location: In the car park of a business enterprise in a converted barn in the village of Castle Rising. Castle Rising has a one-way system so you will find this car park on the right-hand side once around the corner from the pub and church

Facilities: Pub and tea room in the village

Entry Cost: Yes, for Castle Rising Castle, but not for the car park in the village

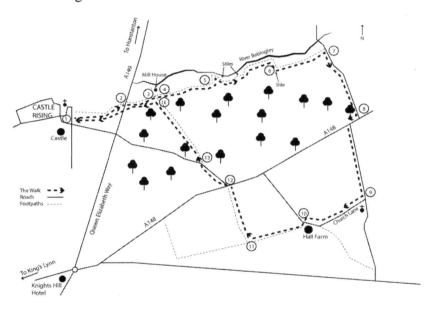

1. Walk out of the car park towards the road. Cross straight over the road walking between a house on your left and a hedge on your right. This brings you to a much narrower path with a yew hedge on the right-hand side and a "country" hedge on the left. This path then brings you out

114

onto open conservation land with wonderful views over the countryside. Follow this obvious path until you reach the main and very busy A149.

2. Cross straight over the main road and head into the wood. You'll see a wooden footpath sign on the edge of the wood. Follow the narrow but obvious path through the woodland, crossing over the little stream, until you reach a large yew hedge at the edge of the wood, a house and a tarmac road.

3. Continue towards the house on the tarmac road.

4. Walk a very short distance to the corner in the road. Here you will see a wide grass track on your right with a footpath sign. Take this path through pretty woodland until you reach a metal gate into an open field at the edge of the woodland.

5. Head diagonally left across this field to the far corner. From here, head into the next field, keeping the river on your left-hand side. Walk over two stiles and through another field until you reach a hedge and metal gate in front of you.

6. Turn right before the hedge and walk to the end of the field where you will see another stile. Once over this stile, turn left and follow the farm track all the way until you reach the tarmac road.

7. At the road, turn right and walk along here until you reach the T junction at the main A148.

8. Turn right and walk along the verge of this road, keeping as far away from the main road as possible. This is the worst part of the walk! About 200 yards along here you'll see a road to the left, signposted to Roydon. Cross over the road and walk in the direction of Roydon.

9. Walk along here until you reach the church. Turn right here (Church Lane) and continue along this country lane until you come to a small triangle and the road bears off to the right. Straight ahead of you is a house.

10. Take the left-hand road and almost immediately on the right is a farmyard and a wooden footpath sign on the fence. Turn right and walk through the farmyard, following this track until you see a wide track on your right lined with a couple of oak trees.

11. Turn right here and walk along this track until you reach the main A148 again (you'll arrive at a beet pad and see a gap in the hedge enabling you to get to the road).

12. Cross straight over the A148 and onto the small lane heading towards the woods. About quarter of a mile along here you will see a stile, a gate and a sign on the fence on the right-hand side.

13. Climb over the stile and follow the woodland track all the way until you reach the yew hedge and the house that you walked past near the beginning of the walk.

14. Just before the tarmac road and the large yew hedge, turn left and retrace your steps back to Castle Rising.

Printed in Great Britain
by Amazon